AN ALPHABET JOURNEY

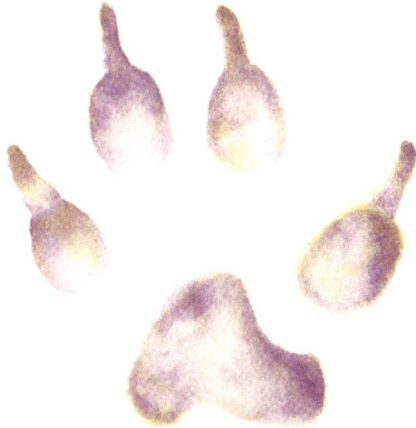

by
Hajra Meeks

Dedicated to all of God's animals, especially the underdogs.

Thank you to my parents, Elijah, Donna, and Kristi. Thanks also to my Kickstarter backers, without which this wouldn't be possible, especially:

Steven Barritz
Jon Christensen
Kimberly Paradis Coryat
Julie Frances Coughlin
Kimberly Hayworth
Liem & Ylan Krueger
Meagan & Brian Molnar & Michael Lafferty
Welda Murphy
Christopher O'Sullivan
Susan Purdin
David Shellenberger
Oliver, Thanya, Bixby & Aqutaq Monstressa Starr

Alone

Bear

Cave

Dream

Endangered

Food

Gun

Highway

Impact

Journey

Kingsnake

Lake

Moon

News

OR-7

Photo

OR-7

Questions

Rabbits

Silent

Transmitter

Uncomfortable

Vulture

Wildfire

Yearning

Oregon

California

X

Zigzag

Continue the Journey: Visit the Interactive Map!

The interactive map at

hajrameeks.com/journey.html

is a supplement to *An Alphabet Journey.* You can follow Journey in a different way on this map-- the book and the map each take you on unique interpretations of the famous gray wolf's trek. You can:

• Mouse over route sections to see where OR-7/Journey travelled in 2012.

• Click on paw prints to learn more.

• You can also click on the vignette buttons below the map to view the terrain and wildlife features.

• Click on the paw print by Marin to meet Aqutaq, an arctic wolf.

• For parent/teacher discussion questions, visit:
hajrameeks.com/discussjourney.html

Here are a few to get you started:

1) E is for 'Endangered.' Is the eagle endangered or is the wolf, or are they both? How should we define endangered?

2) H and I are for 'Highway' and 'Impact.' How do highways impact or affect wildlife? Turn on the highway data on the interactive map. Which highways has Journey been near?

3) Y is for Yearning. What does 'Yearning' mean and how does it relate to Journey zigzagging around the map? Use A for Alone and D for Dream to help explain your answer.

Want more? To create your own OR-7 painting on-line, visit:

hajrameeks.com/journeycolor.html

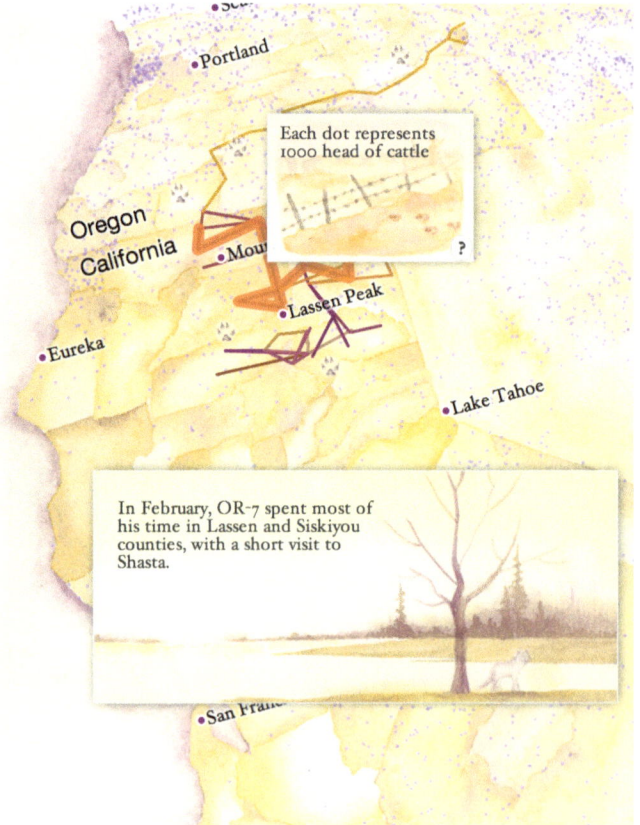

Each dot represents 1000 head of cattle

In February, OR-7 spent most of his time in Lassen and Siskiyou counties, with a short visit to Shasta.

Portland

Oregon
California

Mou

Lassen Peak

Eureka

Lake Tahoe

San Fran

www.ingramcontent.com/pod-product-compliance
Lightning Source LLC
LaVergne TN
LVHW072132070426
835513LV00002B/75